Copyright © 2023 by Herman Strange (Author)

All rights reserved. This book or any portion thereof may not be reproduced or used in any manner whatsoever without the express written permission of the publisher except for the use of brief quotations in a book review.

This book is copyright protected. This is only for personal use. You cannot amend, distributor, sell, use, quote or paraphrase any part or the content within this book without the consent of the author. Please note the information contained within this document is for educational and entertainment purposes only. Every attempt has been made to provide accurate, up to date and reliable complete information. No warranties of any kind are expressed or implied.

Readers acknowledge that the author is not engaging in the rendering of legal, financial, medical or professional advice. The content of this book has been derived from various sources. Please consult a licensed professional before attempting any techniques outlined in this book.

By reading this document, the readers agree that under no circumstances are the author responsible for any losses, direct or indirect, which are incurred as a result of the use of information contained within this document, including but not limited to errors, omissions or inaccuracies.

Thank you very much for reading this book.

Title: Artificial Intelligence and legal-Balancing Efficiency, Fairness, and Accountability
Subtitle: Strategies for Implementing AI in Legal Settings

Author: Herman Strange

Table of Contents

Introduction 6
Definition of artificial intelligence and its applications in law 6
The purpose of the book 9
Brief overview of the chapters 11

Chapter 1: The Basics of AI for Lawyers 14
Overview of AI technologies and their application in the legal industry 14
The benefits of AI for lawyers 17
The challenges of AI adoption in law firms 19
The role of lawyers in developing and implementing AI systems 21

Chapter 2: AI and Legal Research 24
AI-assisted legal research and its benefits 24
Natural language processing and machine learning for legal research 26
The impact of AI on the legal research industry 29
Potential challenges and limitations of AI in legal research 31

Chapter 3: AI and Contract Review 34
AI-assisted contract review and its benefits 34
Use cases for AI in contract review 36
The impact of AI on contract review industry 38

Potential challenges and limitations of AI in contract review 40

Chapter 4: AI and Predictive Analytics in the Legal Industry 43

Overview of predictive analytics and machine learning algorithms for legal predictions 43

The benefits of predictive analytics for the legal industry 47

Legal use cases for predictive analytics and machine learning 50

Potential ethical implications of predictive analytics in law 53

Chapter 5: AI and Intellectual Property Law 56

AI applications in intellectual property law 56

AI-generated inventions and patent law 60

The legal issues surrounding AI-generated content 63

The challenges of regulating AI in intellectual property law 67

Chapter 6: AI and the Future of the Legal Industry 70

The potential future of AI in law 70

The impact of AI on the legal profession and legal education 73

The ethical implications of AI in law 76

Potential challenges and opportunities for the legal industry in the age of AI" the sub topic for about 3000 words long *79*

Conclusion **83**

The potential future of AI in law and its impact on society *83*

The need for continued research and development in AI for law *86*

The importance of ethical and responsible AI development and use in the legal industry *89*

Final thoughts and recommendations for further reading *92*

Potential References **95**

Introduction
Definition of artificial intelligence and its applications in law

Artificial intelligence (AI) has been a hot topic in recent years, and its potential to transform various industries, including the legal sector, has been widely discussed. AI has the ability to automate tasks, analyze data, and make predictions, which can save time and increase efficiency in legal settings. However, it also raises ethical concerns, particularly with respect to bias, accountability, and transparency. In this chapter, we will define what AI is and its applications in law.

Defining AI:

AI refers to computer systems that can perform tasks that would typically require human intelligence, such as learning, problem-solving, and decision-making. AI can be categorized into two types: narrow or weak AI, and general or strong AI. Narrow AI is designed to perform a specific task, such as playing chess or recommending movies based on user preferences. General AI, on the other hand, is designed to perform any intellectual task that a human can, and may be capable of achieving human-level intelligence or beyond.

Applications of AI in Law:

AI has several potential applications in the legal industry, including:

1. Legal Research: AI can assist with legal research by analyzing large volumes of data and identifying relevant information, such as case law and regulations. This can save lawyers time and increase the accuracy of their research.

2. Contract Review: AI can assist with contract review by identifying potential issues and inconsistencies, and providing recommendations for revisions. This can help lawyers ensure that contracts are accurate and enforceable.

3. Predictive Analytics: AI can assist with predictive analytics by analyzing data and making predictions about legal outcomes, such as the likelihood of winning a case or settling a dispute. This can help lawyers make more informed decisions.

4. Intellectual Property Law: AI can assist with intellectual property law by identifying potential patent infringement and copyright violations, and monitoring for unauthorized use of protected works.

In summary, AI refers to computer systems that can perform tasks that would typically require human intelligence. AI has several potential applications in the legal industry, including legal research, contract review, predictive analytics, and intellectual property law. However, the use of

AI in law also raises ethical concerns, which we will explore further in later chapters.

The purpose of the book

Artificial intelligence (AI) has the potential to revolutionize the legal industry by automating tasks, increasing efficiency, and improving accuracy. However, the use of AI in law also raises ethical concerns, particularly with respect to bias, accountability, and transparency. The purpose of this book is to explore the applications of AI in the legal industry, and to discuss strategies for implementing AI in a way that balances efficiency, fairness, and accountability.

The Need for the Book:

As AI continues to advance, it is becoming increasingly important for lawyers, law firms, and legal organizations to understand the potential benefits and risks of AI in the legal industry. While there has been some research on the topic, there is still a need for a comprehensive and accessible guide to AI and its applications in law.

The Purpose of the Book:

The purpose of this book is to provide a comprehensive guide to AI and its applications in the legal industry, and to discuss strategies for implementing AI in a way that balances efficiency, fairness, and accountability. Specifically, this book aims to:

1. Provide an overview of AI technologies and their application in the legal industry.

2. Discuss the benefits and challenges of AI adoption in law firms.

3. Explore the role of lawyers in developing and implementing AI systems.

4. Analyze the impact of AI on legal research, contract review, predictive analytics, and intellectual property law.

5. Discuss the ethical implications of AI in the legal industry.

6. Provide strategies for implementing AI in a way that balances efficiency, fairness, and accountability.

7. Discuss the potential future of AI in law, and its impact on the legal profession and legal education.

In summary, the purpose of this book is to explore the applications of AI in the legal industry, and to provide strategies for implementing AI in a way that balances efficiency, fairness, and accountability. By providing a comprehensive and accessible guide to AI and its applications in law, this book aims to help lawyers, law firms, and legal organizations navigate the ethical and practical implications of AI adoption in the legal industry.

Brief overview of the chapters

This book explores the applications of artificial intelligence (AI) in the legal industry, and provides strategies for implementing AI in a way that balances efficiency, fairness, and accountability. The book is divided into six chapters, each of which covers a specific aspect of AI in law. In this section, we provide a brief overview of each chapter.

Chapter 1: The Basics of AI for Lawyers

This chapter provides an overview of AI technologies and their application in the legal industry. It discusses the benefits of AI for lawyers, as well as the challenges of AI adoption in law firms. The chapter also explores the role of lawyers in developing and implementing AI systems.

Chapter 2: AI and Legal Research

This chapter focuses on AI-assisted legal research and its benefits. It discusses the use of natural language processing and machine learning for legal research, and analyzes the impact of AI on the legal research industry. The chapter also discusses potential challenges and limitations of AI in legal research.

Chapter 3: AI and Contract Review

This chapter explores AI-assisted contract review and its benefits. It discusses use cases for AI in contract review, and analyzes the impact of AI on the contract review industry. The chapter also discusses potential challenges and limitations of AI in contract review.

Chapter 4: AI and Predictive Analytics in the Legal Industry

This chapter provides an overview of predictive analytics and machine learning algorithms for legal predictions. It discusses the benefits of predictive analytics for the legal industry, as well as legal use cases for predictive analytics and machine learning. The chapter also discusses potential ethical implications of predictive analytics in law.

Chapter 5: AI and Intellectual Property Law

This chapter focuses on AI applications in intellectual property law. It discusses AI-generated inventions and patent law, as well as the legal issues surrounding AI-generated content. The chapter also explores the challenges of regulating AI in intellectual property law.

Chapter 6: AI and the Future of the Legal Industry

This chapter discusses the potential future of AI in law, and its impact on the legal profession and legal education. It analyzes the ethical implications of AI in law, and provides strategies for implementing AI in a way that balances efficiency, fairness, and accountability. The chapter also discusses potential challenges and opportunities for the legal industry in the age of AI.

Conclusion:

In conclusion, this book provides a comprehensive guide to AI and its applications in the legal industry. By exploring the benefits and challenges of AI adoption in law firms, and providing strategies for implementing AI in a way that balances efficiency, fairness, and accountability, this book aims to help lawyers, law firms, and legal organizations navigate the ethical and practical implications of AI in law.

Chapter 1: The Basics of AI for Lawyers
Overview of AI technologies and their application in the legal industry

Artificial intelligence (AI) technologies are transforming the legal industry by automating tasks that previously required human intervention. These technologies use algorithms, natural language processing, and machine learning to analyze data and make predictions based on patterns and insights that are difficult for humans to recognize. The legal industry has been slow to adopt AI technologies, but there are several applications that are gaining traction. In this section, we will provide an overview of AI technologies and their application in the legal industry.

Document review and analysis

One of the most promising applications of AI in the legal industry is document review and analysis. AI-powered document review software can analyze large volumes of documents and identify relevant information, such as key phrases, concepts, and entities. This technology can save lawyers significant amounts of time and money by automating tasks that would otherwise require extensive manual review.

Legal research

Another application of AI in the legal industry is legal research. Legal research can be time-consuming and labor-intensive, but AI-powered legal research tools can help lawyers quickly find relevant cases, statutes, and regulations. These tools use natural language processing and machine learning to analyze large volumes of legal data and identify relevant information.

Case prediction

AI technologies can also be used for case prediction, which involves using historical data to predict the outcomes of future cases. Predictive analytics tools use machine learning algorithms to analyze past cases and identify patterns that can be used to predict the outcomes of new cases. This technology can help lawyers make more informed decisions about which cases to take on and how to approach them.

Contract analysis

AI technologies can also be used for contract analysis, which involves reviewing and analyzing legal contracts. Contract analysis tools use natural language processing and machine learning to identify key terms and clauses, flag potential risks, and identify areas for improvement. This technology can help lawyers draft better contracts, negotiate more effectively, and reduce the risk of legal disputes.

Legal chatbots

Finally, AI technologies can be used to develop legal chatbots, which can assist with basic legal tasks such as answering frequently asked questions and providing legal advice. Legal chatbots use natural language processing to understand user queries and provide relevant responses. While chatbots are not a substitute for human lawyers, they can provide basic legal services at a lower cost and with greater efficiency.

Conclusion:

AI technologies are transforming the legal industry by automating tasks that were previously performed manually. These technologies are making legal services more efficient, accurate, and cost-effective. While the legal industry has been slow to adopt AI, there are several promising applications that are gaining traction. In the following chapters, we will explore these applications in greater detail and provide strategies for implementing AI in a way that balances efficiency, fairness, and accountability.

The benefits of AI for lawyers

Artificial intelligence (AI) has the potential to revolutionize the legal industry, providing lawyers with powerful tools for legal research, contract analysis, and predictive analytics. The benefits of AI for lawyers are numerous and significant, and include:

1. Increased efficiency and productivity: AI tools can help lawyers automate many time-consuming tasks, such as document review and contract analysis. This can free up time for lawyers to focus on more complex tasks and provide greater value to their clients.

2. Improved accuracy: AI tools can analyze vast amounts of data with greater speed and accuracy than humans, reducing the risk of errors and improving the quality of legal work.

3. Enhanced decision-making: AI tools can provide lawyers with insights and analysis that can inform their decision-making, allowing them to make more informed and strategic choices.

4. Cost savings: By automating many routine legal tasks, AI can help firms reduce their overhead costs and increase profitability.

5. Competitive advantage: Firms that adopt AI tools and technologies can gain a competitive edge by providing

clients with faster, more accurate, and more cost-effective legal services.

6. Improved client satisfaction: By using AI tools to streamline legal processes and improve the quality of their work, lawyers can provide clients with a better overall experience and strengthen their relationships with them.

Overall, the benefits of AI for lawyers are clear. AI has the potential to transform the legal industry by improving efficiency, accuracy, and decision-making, while reducing costs and enhancing the client experience. However, it is important for lawyers to understand the limitations and challenges of AI adoption, and to develop strategies for integrating AI tools into their practices in a way that maximizes their benefits and minimizes their risks.

The challenges of AI adoption in law firms

While there are numerous benefits to using artificial intelligence (AI) tools in the legal industry, there are also a number of challenges that law firms may face when trying to adopt these technologies. Some of the key challenges of AI adoption in law firms include:

1. Technical complexity: AI technologies can be complex and require specialized expertise to develop, implement, and maintain. Many law firms may lack the technical expertise and resources needed to effectively integrate these tools into their workflows.

2. Cost: AI technologies can be expensive to develop and implement, particularly for smaller firms with limited budgets. This can create barriers to adoption, especially for firms that may not have a clear understanding of the return on investment (ROI) of these technologies.

3. Resistance to change: Some lawyers may be hesitant to adopt new technologies, particularly if they feel that these tools could threaten their job security or professional autonomy. This can create resistance to change within the firm and make it more difficult to implement new technologies.

4. Lack of standardization: There are currently no universal standards for AI in the legal industry, which can

make it difficult to compare and evaluate different tools and technologies. This can create confusion and uncertainty for firms trying to select and implement these technologies.

5. Ethical concerns: There are a number of ethical concerns related to the use of AI in the legal industry, including issues related to bias, privacy, and transparency. Law firms may need to develop strategies for addressing these concerns and ensuring that their use of AI tools is ethical and responsible.

6. Data quality: AI tools rely on high-quality data to be effective, and many law firms may not have access to the high-quality data needed to train these tools. This can limit the effectiveness of AI tools and make it more difficult to achieve the desired results.

Overall, the challenges of AI adoption in law firms are significant, and firms will need to be strategic in their approach to implementing these technologies. Addressing these challenges will require a combination of technical expertise, financial investment, and a willingness to embrace change. Firms that are able to successfully navigate these challenges, however, stand to reap significant benefits from the use of AI tools in their legal practice.

The role of lawyers in developing and implementing AI systems

As AI becomes increasingly prevalent in the legal industry, it is important for lawyers to understand their role in the development and implementation of these systems. This includes not only ensuring that AI is used effectively and ethically, but also advocating for its adoption within their firms and organizations.

One of the most important roles that lawyers can play in developing and implementing AI systems is in defining the legal requirements and constraints of these systems. This includes working with software developers and data scientists to ensure that the algorithms used in AI systems comply with legal regulations and ethical standards. It also includes defining the types of data that can be used in these systems, as well as the criteria for evaluating the accuracy and fairness of the results they produce.

Another important role for lawyers is to help ensure that AI systems are transparent and explainable. This is particularly important in legal contexts, where decisions made by AI systems may have significant consequences for individuals and organizations. Lawyers can help ensure that these systems are designed in a way that allows their decision-making processes to be understood and scrutinized.

Lawyers can also play a critical role in the adoption of AI systems within law firms and other organizations. This includes advocating for the use of these systems, helping to train colleagues on their use, and working to build support for their adoption. Lawyers can also help to identify the types of legal tasks that are most amenable to AI automation, and to develop strategies for integrating these systems into legal workflows.

Of course, there are also challenges associated with the role of lawyers in developing and implementing AI systems. One of the biggest challenges is simply keeping up with the rapid pace of technological change in this field. Lawyers must be willing to invest time and effort into staying informed about the latest developments in AI technology, and to work collaboratively with data scientists and software developers to ensure that AI systems are being used effectively and ethically.

Another challenge is navigating the ethical and legal issues that arise when AI systems are used in legal contexts. Lawyers must be sensitive to the potential for bias and discrimination in these systems, and work to ensure that they are used in ways that are fair and equitable. They must also be aware of the legal and regulatory constraints on AI use, and work to ensure that AI systems comply with these requirements.

Overall, the role of lawyers in developing and implementing AI systems is an important one, and will become increasingly critical as AI becomes more prevalent in the legal industry. By working collaboratively with data scientists and software developers, and by advocating for the ethical and responsible use of AI, lawyers can help to ensure that these systems are used to their full potential in the legal industry.

Chapter 2: AI and Legal Research

AI-assisted legal research and its benefits

AI-assisted legal research refers to the use of artificial intelligence technology to help legal professionals search, analyze, and review legal information more efficiently and accurately. AI has the potential to revolutionize the legal research process by offering a wide range of benefits.

One of the most significant benefits of AI-assisted legal research is its ability to save time and increase efficiency. With the help of AI-powered tools, legal researchers can automate the process of searching for and reviewing legal documents, freeing up time for lawyers to focus on more complex tasks. AI algorithms can also identify relevant case law, statutes, and regulations, allowing lawyers to quickly assess the strengths and weaknesses of their arguments.

AI-assisted legal research can also help lawyers identify patterns and insights that might be missed through traditional research methods. AI algorithms can analyze vast amounts of legal data and identify connections between cases, laws, and regulations that may not be immediately apparent to human researchers. This can help lawyers build stronger arguments and anticipate potential legal issues.

Another benefit of AI-assisted legal research is its ability to improve accuracy and reduce errors. Legal research is a time-consuming and complex process that requires a high level of attention to detail. However, it's easy for even the most experienced researchers to miss important information. AI tools can help ensure that legal professionals don't miss anything significant by cross-referencing and verifying information across multiple sources.

AI-powered legal research tools can also help reduce costs for law firms and clients. By automating the research process and improving accuracy, legal professionals can save time and resources. This can translate into lower costs for clients and increased profitability for law firms.

In summary, AI-assisted legal research offers a range of benefits, including increased efficiency, improved accuracy, and reduced costs. By utilizing AI-powered tools, legal professionals can streamline the research process and gain valuable insights into legal issues that might otherwise be overlooked. As the legal industry continues to evolve, AI will undoubtedly play an increasingly significant role in legal research and practice.

Natural language processing and machine learning for legal research

Natural language processing (NLP) and machine learning (ML) are two of the most important branches of artificial intelligence that have revolutionized legal research. NLP is a subfield of AI that focuses on the interaction between human language and computers. It enables computers to understand, interpret, and generate human language. ML, on the other hand, is a technique that enables computers to learn from data and improve their performance without being explicitly programmed.

When applied to legal research, NLP and ML technologies can analyze vast amounts of legal texts, extract relevant information, and provide valuable insights to legal professionals. Here are some ways NLP and ML are used for legal research:

1. Document Classification: NLP can be used to classify legal documents such as case briefs, court opinions, and contracts. This can help lawyers find relevant information quickly and efficiently.

2. Entity Extraction: NLP can identify entities mentioned in legal documents, such as names of people, organizations, and locations. This can help lawyers track

legal entities, such as clients or opposing parties, and uncover connections between them.

3. Sentiment Analysis: NLP can determine the sentiment or emotional tone of legal documents. This can help lawyers understand the attitude of judges, juries, or witnesses, and adjust their arguments accordingly.

4. Legal Language Processing: Legal language can be complex and difficult to understand for non-lawyers. NLP can simplify legal language by summarizing, paraphrasing, or translating legal texts into plain language.

ML, on the other hand, can learn from large datasets of legal documents and make predictions or recommendations based on this data. For example:

1. Legal Prediction: ML algorithms can analyze large datasets of past legal cases to predict the outcome of new cases. This can help lawyers assess the risks and benefits of pursuing a legal action.

2. Legal Recommendation: ML algorithms can recommend legal documents or case law that are relevant to a specific legal question. This can help lawyers save time and resources by providing them with the most relevant information.

NLP and ML have numerous benefits for legal research. They can save time, reduce costs, and improve the accuracy of legal research. However, there are also some challenges associated with using NLP and ML in legal research, such as bias, accuracy, and transparency. These challenges must be addressed to ensure that the benefits of AI are fully realized in the legal industry.

The impact of AI on the legal research industry

Artificial intelligence is revolutionizing the way legal research is conducted, and the impact is significant. AI tools can streamline and automate many of the time-consuming and tedious tasks that legal researchers must perform, enabling them to work more efficiently and effectively.

One of the most significant impacts of AI on the legal research industry is the ability to process large amounts of data quickly and accurately. Legal research has traditionally been a labor-intensive process, involving reading through thousands of pages of legal documents, searching through databases, and manually extracting relevant information. With AI, researchers can leverage machine learning algorithms to quickly scan vast quantities of data and identify relevant information with a high degree of accuracy.

Another significant impact of AI on the legal research industry is the ability to improve the quality and accuracy of research. Natural language processing (NLP) is a form of AI that enables computers to understand human language and translate it into a structured format that can be analyzed. NLP allows legal researchers to conduct more nuanced searches, identify relevant case law, and extract key legal concepts and arguments from large volumes of text.

AI tools can also help legal researchers identify relevant documents more quickly and accurately. For example, machine learning algorithms can analyze the language and structure of legal documents and identify key clauses, provisions, and concepts. This can save researchers a significant amount of time, allowing them to focus on more complex legal issues.

One of the most significant impacts of AI on the legal research industry is the ability to democratize access to legal information. In the past, legal research was largely the domain of large law firms and corporations, which had the resources to hire teams of researchers and access expensive databases. With AI-powered legal research tools, smaller firms and solo practitioners can access the same level of legal research capabilities, helping to level the playing field and promote greater access to justice.

Overall, the impact of AI on the legal research industry is significant, and the benefits are clear. AI tools can save legal researchers time and improve the quality and accuracy of their work, while also democratizing access to legal information. As AI continues to evolve, it is likely that we will see even more significant impacts on the legal industry in the years to come.

Potential challenges and limitations of AI in legal research

AI-assisted legal research has many benefits, but there are also potential challenges and limitations that must be considered. In this section, we will explore some of these challenges and limitations.

1. Bias in AI

One of the most significant challenges of using AI in legal research is the potential for bias. AI systems are only as unbiased as the data they are trained on. If the data used to train the system is biased, then the system will produce biased results. This can have serious consequences, particularly in the legal field, where decisions based on inaccurate or biased information can have long-lasting effects.

2. Lack of transparency

AI systems can be complex and difficult to understand, even for experts in the field. This lack of transparency can be a significant limitation in legal research, as lawyers and judges need to understand how the system arrived at its conclusion in order to make informed decisions. Lack of transparency can also make it difficult to identify errors or biases in the system.

3. Quality of data

The accuracy and reliability of AI systems depend on the quality of the data they are trained on. If the data is incomplete, outdated, or inaccurate, the system will produce flawed results. In the legal field, it can be challenging to obtain high-quality data, as legal cases can be complex, and the data can be dispersed across many sources.

4. Ethical concerns

AI raises many ethical concerns in legal research. For example, who is responsible for the decisions made by the AI system? How can the rights of individuals be protected when AI systems are used to process personal data? How can the use of AI be reconciled with principles of fairness and equality?

5. Limitations of AI

While AI has the potential to improve legal research, there are still limitations to what AI can do. AI systems are not capable of understanding context, human emotions, or the nuances of language in the way that humans can. This can make it difficult for AI systems to provide a complete analysis of legal issues.

6. Cost and access

AI systems can be expensive to develop and implement, which can limit their use to larger law firms and organizations. This can create a disadvantage for smaller firms or individuals who may not have access to these tools.

7. Need for human expertise

AI systems can assist in legal research, but they cannot replace the need for human expertise. Lawyers and legal professionals will still be needed to interpret and apply the results produced by the AI system. Therefore, it is essential that lawyers have the necessary training and expertise to work with these tools effectively.

In conclusion, AI has the potential to revolutionize legal research, but there are also potential challenges and limitations that must be addressed. By understanding these challenges and working to overcome them, legal professionals can harness the power of AI to provide more accurate, efficient, and effective legal research.

Chapter 3: AI and Contract Review
AI-assisted contract review and its benefits

AI-assisted contract review is a rapidly growing field that has the potential to significantly improve the efficiency and accuracy of contract analysis. In this chapter, we will explore the benefits of AI in contract review and how it can help lawyers and businesses save time and money while minimizing the risk of errors.

One of the primary benefits of AI in contract review is its ability to quickly identify key provisions and clauses in contracts. AI algorithms can be trained to recognize specific language patterns and extract information from large volumes of text, allowing lawyers to quickly identify important terms and clauses without having to manually review each contract.

Another benefit of AI in contract review is its ability to identify potential legal risks and issues. AI algorithms can be trained to flag specific language that may indicate legal risks or potential issues, such as clauses that are unenforceable or violate legal requirements.

AI can also help identify inconsistencies or errors in contracts, which can be difficult and time-consuming for human lawyers to catch. By using machine learning algorithms, AI systems can quickly identify and flag inconsistencies in contracts and suggest revisions or amendments to improve the overall quality of the document.

Furthermore, AI can also help lawyers and businesses manage and analyze large volumes of contracts more efficiently. With the use of AI, companies can quickly search and retrieve specific contract terms and provisions, enabling them to make informed decisions and take appropriate action more quickly.

Overall, AI-assisted contract review offers numerous benefits for lawyers and businesses, including increased efficiency, improved accuracy, and reduced risk. By leveraging the power of AI, lawyers can save valuable time and resources and focus on more high-level tasks, while businesses can better manage and mitigate their legal risks.

Use cases for AI in contract review

AI technology has shown significant potential in contract review processes, offering various use cases for the legal industry. Here are some of the most promising use cases for AI in contract review:

1. Contract Analysis: AI can analyze large volumes of contracts, extracting specific provisions and clauses, identifying key terms, and summarizing the content of the agreement. This enables lawyers to review contracts more quickly and accurately and helps them identify potential risks and opportunities.

2. Due Diligence: In M&A transactions or other business deals, lawyers need to review large numbers of contracts to assess potential liabilities and risks. AI can help automate due diligence by quickly reviewing contracts and identifying potential issues, such as non-compliant clauses or missing provisions.

3. Contract Management: AI-powered contract management systems can automatically store and organize contracts, track key deadlines, and send alerts when certain events occur. This helps companies stay on top of their contracts and reduces the risk of missing important deadlines or obligations.

4. Contract Standardization: Many companies have numerous templates for contracts, which can lead to inconsistencies and errors. AI can help standardize contracts by identifying common clauses, terms, and conditions and recommending changes to create more consistent contracts.

5. Compliance Monitoring: AI can help monitor contracts for compliance with laws and regulations. By analyzing contracts and comparing them to relevant laws, regulations, and policies, AI can identify potential compliance issues and help lawyers take appropriate actions.

6. Contract Generation: AI-powered contract generation tools can create contracts from scratch, based on predefined templates and clauses. This saves time for lawyers and reduces the risk of errors and inconsistencies.

Overall, AI offers significant benefits in contract review processes, helping lawyers save time, reduce errors, and identify potential risks and opportunities.

The impact of AI on contract review industry

The impact of AI on the contract review industry is significant and can be seen in several ways. AI-assisted contract review has the potential to revolutionize the way contracts are reviewed, managed, and executed. Here are some of the key impacts of AI on the contract review industry:

1. Increased efficiency and speed: AI technology can automate contract review tasks that would otherwise take hours or even days for a human to complete. With AI, contracts can be reviewed and analyzed in a matter of minutes or even seconds, which can save significant amounts of time and improve overall efficiency.

2. Improved accuracy and consistency: AI can help ensure that contract review is consistent and accurate, reducing the risk of errors or omissions. AI can also help identify inconsistencies or anomalies in contracts that might be missed by human reviewers, improving the quality of contract review.

3. Cost savings: AI-assisted contract review can significantly reduce the cost of reviewing and managing contracts. This can be especially beneficial for small and medium-sized businesses that may not have the resources to hire dedicated legal teams to manage their contracts.

4. Enhanced risk management: AI can help identify potential risks in contracts and flag them for further review or action. This can help organizations manage their risk exposure and ensure compliance with relevant laws and regulations.

5. Improved decision-making: With AI, organizations can quickly analyze large amounts of contract data and extract insights that can inform strategic decision-making. This can help organizations identify opportunities for cost savings, negotiate better contract terms, and improve overall business performance.

Overall, the impact of AI on the contract review industry is largely positive, with the potential to improve efficiency, accuracy, and cost-effectiveness. However, there are also some challenges associated with AI adoption in contract review, including data privacy concerns and the need to ensure that AI systems are transparent and explainable.

Potential challenges and limitations of AI in contract review

As with any technology, AI in contract review is not without its challenges and limitations. In this section, we will explore some of the potential issues that may arise when using AI for contract review.

1. Data quality and bias One of the biggest concerns with using AI for contract review is the quality of data used to train the algorithms. If the data is incomplete, outdated, or biased, it can affect the accuracy and fairness of the results. This can lead to errors or inconsistencies in the contract review process, which can ultimately undermine its reliability.

To mitigate this risk, it is important to ensure that the data used to train AI algorithms is representative and unbiased. This may require the use of diverse datasets, as well as the use of techniques such as data cleaning and preprocessing to remove bias and ensure the accuracy of the data.

2. Lack of interpretability Another challenge with AI in contract review is the lack of interpretability of the results. In many cases, the algorithms used in AI systems are complex and difficult to understand, making it challenging

for lawyers to interpret and explain the results to clients or other stakeholders.

To address this issue, researchers are developing new techniques for explaining AI results, such as visualizations and natural language explanations. Additionally, some experts are calling for greater transparency and accountability in AI systems, which could help increase the interpretability of the results.

3. Limited scope of AI systems While AI has the potential to revolutionize contract review, there are some limitations to what AI can accomplish. For example, AI may struggle with understanding the nuances of legal language or context, which can limit its effectiveness in certain areas of contract review.

To address this challenge, some experts are exploring the use of hybrid systems that combine AI with human expertise. By leveraging the strengths of both humans and machines, these systems can provide a more comprehensive and accurate assessment of contracts.

4. Ethics and privacy concerns Finally, the use of AI in contract review raises a number of ethical and privacy concerns. For example, there may be concerns around the use of personal data or the potential for bias or discrimination in the results.

To mitigate these risks, it is important to establish clear ethical guidelines and standards for the use of AI in contract review. This may include establishing protocols for data privacy and security, as well as ensuring that the algorithms used in AI systems are transparent and unbiased.

In conclusion, while there are certainly challenges and limitations associated with the use of AI in contract review, these issues can be addressed with careful planning, attention to data quality, and a commitment to ethical and transparent practices. Ultimately, AI has the potential to transform the contract review industry, making it faster, more accurate, and more efficient than ever before.

Chapter 4: AI and Predictive Analytics in the Legal Industry

Overview of predictive analytics and machine learning algorithms for legal predictions

Predictive analytics and machine learning algorithms have become increasingly popular in the legal industry to improve decision-making and predict outcomes. Predictive analytics involves using historical data to make predictions about future events, and machine learning algorithms use these predictions to continuously learn and improve their accuracy over time.

In the legal industry, predictive analytics and machine learning algorithms can be used in a variety of applications, including case outcome prediction, risk analysis, and document review. For example, predictive analytics can help lawyers assess the likelihood of success in a case and develop strategies accordingly. Similarly, risk analysis can be used to identify potential areas of legal exposure and develop risk management strategies.

Machine learning algorithms are particularly effective in legal applications because they can identify patterns and correlations in large amounts of data that may not be apparent to human analysts. Additionally, machine learning algorithms can learn from new data and adjust their predictions accordingly, making them a powerful tool for ongoing analysis.

Case Outcome Prediction

One of the most common applications of predictive analytics in the legal industry is case outcome prediction. By analyzing data from previous cases, machine learning algorithms can identify patterns and factors that are predictive of case outcomes. This data can then be used to predict the likelihood of success in a new case.

Case outcome prediction can be useful for a variety of legal professionals, including litigators, judges, and clients. Litigators can use case outcome predictions to develop case strategies and negotiate settlements, while judges can use predictions to inform their decisions. Clients can use predictions to make informed decisions about whether to pursue litigation.

However, it is important to note that case outcome prediction is not always accurate, and the use of predictive analytics in legal decision-making is still relatively new. As such, it is important for legal professionals to use predictive analytics in conjunction with their own expertise and judgement.

Risk Analysis

Another application of predictive analytics in the legal industry is risk analysis. By analyzing data on past legal issues, machine learning algorithms can identify areas of legal exposure and predict the likelihood of future legal issues.

Risk analysis can be particularly useful for businesses, as it can help them identify areas of legal risk and develop risk management strategies. For example, a company might use risk analysis to identify areas where they are most likely to face lawsuits, such as product liability or employment law issues. They can then develop strategies to mitigate these risks, such as improving product safety or implementing policies to reduce the risk of employment law violations.

Document Review

Predictive analytics can also be used in document review, particularly in cases with large volumes of data. Machine learning algorithms can analyze documents and identify relevant information, allowing lawyers to quickly review large amounts of data and identify key pieces of information.

Document review can be particularly useful in e-discovery, where large volumes of electronic data must be reviewed for relevant information. By using predictive analytics to identify relevant documents, lawyers can save time and reduce the cost of e-discovery.

Conclusion

Predictive analytics and machine learning algorithms have the potential to revolutionize the legal industry by improving decision-making and predicting outcomes. While these technologies are still relatively new in the legal industry, their potential benefits are significant. However, it is important for legal professionals to use predictive analytics in conjunction with their own expertise and judgement, and to be aware of the potential limitations and challenges of these technologies.

The benefits of predictive analytics for the legal industry

The use of predictive analytics in the legal industry can have significant benefits, ranging from improving accuracy in legal predictions to increasing efficiency in legal operations. Here are some of the main benefits of predictive analytics for the legal industry:

1. Improved accuracy in legal predictions: Predictive analytics can help lawyers make more accurate predictions about the outcomes of legal cases. By analyzing data from past cases, predictive analytics algorithms can identify patterns and trends that can be used to predict the likelihood of certain outcomes in future cases. This can help lawyers make better-informed decisions about how to approach a case and can ultimately lead to better outcomes for clients.

2. Increased efficiency in legal operations: Predictive analytics can also help law firms operate more efficiently by automating certain tasks and reducing the need for manual review of large amounts of data. For example, predictive analytics algorithms can be used to analyze large volumes of documents and contracts in order to identify key information or potential issues. This can save lawyers time and effort, allowing them to focus on more complex and high-value tasks.

3. Improved risk management: Predictive analytics can help lawyers and law firms better manage risk by identifying potential risks before they become a problem. For example, predictive analytics algorithms can be used to analyze financial data and identify patterns that may indicate fraud or other financial crimes. This can help lawyers and law firms take proactive steps to mitigate risk and avoid potential legal issues.

4. Enhanced decision-making: Predictive analytics can also help lawyers make more informed decisions by providing them with data-driven insights. By analyzing data from past cases and legal trends, predictive analytics algorithms can help lawyers identify key factors that may impact the outcome of a case. This can help lawyers make better-informed decisions about how to approach a case and can ultimately lead to better outcomes for clients.

5. Competitive advantage: Finally, the use of predictive analytics can provide law firms with a competitive advantage by enabling them to provide more accurate and efficient legal services to clients. By leveraging the power of data and analytics, law firms can differentiate themselves from their competitors and attract new clients who are looking for more innovative and technology-driven legal services.

Overall, the use of predictive analytics in the legal industry can have significant benefits for both lawyers and their clients. By improving accuracy, increasing efficiency, enhancing risk management, enabling better decision-making, and providing a competitive advantage, predictive analytics can help lawyers deliver more value to their clients and improve their bottom line.

Legal use cases for predictive analytics and machine learning

Legal professionals are increasingly using predictive analytics and machine learning techniques to gain insights into legal data and to make more informed decisions. The following are some use cases for predictive analytics in the legal industry:

1. Predictive analytics for litigation: Litigation is one of the most complex and costly areas of the law. Predictive analytics can help lawyers predict the outcome of cases by analyzing past cases and identifying patterns that may impact the outcome of a particular case. By analyzing factors such as judge history, jurisdiction, and case law, predictive analytics can help lawyers make better decisions about whether to pursue a case or settle out of court.

2. Contract management: Legal professionals can use predictive analytics to identify patterns and risks in contracts, such as potential breaches or areas of non-compliance. Predictive analytics can also be used to predict which contracts are most likely to be profitable and which may pose a risk to a company's bottom line.

3. Regulatory compliance: Predictive analytics can help companies stay compliant with ever-changing regulations by analyzing data on regulatory trends and

identifying potential areas of risk. Legal professionals can use predictive analytics to identify trends in regulatory enforcement, track compliance with regulatory requirements, and identify potential areas of non-compliance.

4. Intellectual property: Predictive analytics can help lawyers predict the outcome of intellectual property disputes by analyzing data on past disputes and identifying patterns that may impact the outcome of a particular case. By analyzing factors such as patent history, technology trends, and competitor activity, predictive analytics can help lawyers make more informed decisions about how to protect their clients' intellectual property.

5. Risk assessment: Predictive analytics can help lawyers assess the risk of certain legal actions by analyzing data on past cases and identifying patterns that may impact the outcome of a particular case. By analyzing factors such as case law, legal precedent, and jurisdictional trends, predictive analytics can help lawyers make more informed decisions about how to proceed with a particular case.

6. E-discovery: Predictive analytics can help lawyers identify relevant documents and data in e-discovery by analyzing patterns in the data and predicting which documents are most relevant to a particular case. This can

help lawyers save time and reduce costs associated with e-discovery.

Overall, predictive analytics and machine learning have the potential to revolutionize the legal industry by helping lawyers make more informed decisions, reducing costs, and increasing efficiency. However, it is important to note that predictive analytics is not a substitute for legal expertise, and should be used in conjunction with traditional legal analysis.

Potential ethical implications of predictive analytics in law

As with any technology, the use of predictive analytics in the legal industry raises potential ethical concerns. In this section, we will explore some of the most significant ethical implications of predictive analytics and machine learning in law.

1. Bias and discrimination: One of the biggest concerns with predictive analytics in law is the potential for bias and discrimination. Predictive models rely on historical data to make predictions about future outcomes, and if that historical data is biased, the model will be biased as well. For example, if historical data shows that people from a certain race or gender are more likely to be convicted of a crime, a predictive model trained on that data may also predict that people from that race or gender are more likely to commit crimes, perpetuating a cycle of bias and discrimination.

2. Privacy: Predictive analytics relies on large amounts of data, often including personal information about individuals. There is a risk that this data could be misused or mishandled, leading to privacy violations. Additionally, there is a risk that individuals could be unfairly targeted or penalized based on their data.

3. Lack of transparency: Predictive analytics models can be complex and difficult to understand, even for experts in the field. This lack of transparency can make it difficult to understand how decisions are being made, and to identify and correct errors or biases.

4. Overreliance on technology: Another concern is the potential for overreliance on predictive analytics and machine learning, which could lead to a lack of critical thinking and judgment. Lawyers and judges should not blindly accept the output of a predictive model without considering other factors and exercising independent judgment.

5. Legal and ethical responsibilities: Lawyers and legal professionals have a duty to act in the best interests of their clients and uphold the ethical standards of the profession. The use of predictive analytics in law raises questions about the ethical and legal responsibilities of lawyers and legal professionals when it comes to using and interpreting the output of these models.

6. Lack of regulation: Finally, there is a lack of clear regulation and oversight when it comes to the use of predictive analytics in the legal industry. This can make it difficult to ensure that ethical standards are being upheld and that individuals are being treated fairly.

In conclusion, while predictive analytics and machine learning hold great promise for the legal industry, there are also significant ethical implications that must be addressed. It is important that lawyers and legal professionals remain aware of these implications and take steps to ensure that the use of predictive analytics is fair, transparent, and in line with ethical standards.

Chapter 5: AI and Intellectual Property Law

AI applications in intellectual property law

Artificial intelligence (AI) has become a game-changer in the field of intellectual property (IP) law. From patent applications to trademark disputes, AI is transforming the way IP law is practiced. Here are some of the most significant AI applications in IP law:

1. Patent Applications: AI is being used to assist with drafting patent applications, which can be a time-consuming and challenging process. AI-powered tools can review prior art and suggest language for patent claims, making the process more efficient and accurate.

2. Trademark Searches: AI-powered trademark search tools can quickly identify similar trademarks and help identify potential conflicts. These tools can also assist with monitoring and tracking trademark applications.

3. Copyright Infringement: AI is being used to detect copyright infringement by scanning online content and comparing it to existing copyrights. This can help content creators and owners protect their IP rights and identify potential infringements.

4. IP Litigation: AI-powered legal analytics tools can help lawyers assess the strengths and weaknesses of their case and predict outcomes. This can help lawyers develop

better litigation strategies and improve their chances of success.

5. IP Portfolio Management: AI can be used to manage large IP portfolios, including identifying potential licensing opportunities, monitoring and enforcing IP rights, and identifying potential infringements.

Benefits of AI in Intellectual Property Law

AI is transforming the field of IP law in many ways, offering numerous benefits to lawyers and clients alike:

1. Increased Efficiency: AI-powered tools can automate time-consuming tasks such as document review and patent application drafting, allowing lawyers to focus on higher-value work.

2. Improved Accuracy: AI can improve the accuracy of patent searches, trademark searches, and copyright infringement detection, reducing the risk of errors and false positives.

3. Cost Savings: AI can help reduce legal costs by automating routine tasks and providing better insights into IP portfolios, allowing lawyers to make more informed decisions.

4. Enhanced Client Service: AI can help lawyers provide better service to clients by providing more accurate

and timely information, improving the speed and quality of legal advice.

5. Competitive Advantage: Law firms that adopt AI early can gain a competitive advantage by offering faster, more accurate, and more cost-effective legal services.

Challenges of AI in Intellectual Property Law

Despite the many benefits of AI in IP law, there are also some challenges to consider:

1. Bias: AI-powered tools can be biased based on the data they are trained on, which can lead to incorrect results. For example, a trademark search tool trained on a dataset that over-represents certain industries may miss relevant trademarks in other industries.

2. Interpretability: AI-powered tools can be difficult to interpret, making it hard to understand how they arrived at their conclusions. This can make it challenging to explain legal decisions to clients or judges.

3. Privacy and Data Security: AI requires large amounts of data to train algorithms, which can raise privacy and data security concerns. Law firms must ensure that client data is properly protected and that AI-powered tools comply with privacy regulations.

4. Legal Ethics: The use of AI in IP law raises ethical questions, such as whether AI tools can replace human

judgment and whether lawyers have an obligation to disclose the use of AI to clients.

Conclusion

AI is transforming the field of IP law, offering significant benefits in terms of efficiency, accuracy, and cost savings. However, there are also challenges to consider, including bias, interpretability, privacy, data security, and legal ethics. As AI continues to evolve, it will be important for lawyers and law firms to stay up-to-date with the latest developments and ensure that their use of AI complies with legal and ethical standards.

AI-generated inventions and patent law

The rapid advancement of AI technology has led to the development of machine learning algorithms that can create new inventions without human intervention. These AI-generated inventions raise unique legal issues in the field of patent law, as they challenge the traditional concept of inventorship and the criteria for patentability.

Inventorship is a fundamental principle in patent law, as only inventors or their assigns can apply for a patent. The patent law defines an inventor as an individual who contributes to the conception of the invention. The concept of conception requires a mental act of invention, which involves the exercise of human creativity, judgment, and ingenuity. The question arises whether an AI system can be considered an inventor under the patent law, given that it lacks consciousness, creativity, and judgment.

The issue of AI-generated inventions was brought to the forefront of the legal debate by the case of DABUS (Device for the Autonomous Bootstrapping of Unified Sentience), an AI system that generated two patent applications for inventions in the field of food containers and flashing lights. The applications were filed by Dr. Stephen Thaler, the creator of DABUS, who argued that the AI system should be recognized as the inventor. The US Patent and

Trademark Office (USPTO) and the European Patent Office (EPO) rejected the applications on the ground that the inventorship requirement can only be satisfied by a natural person.

The DABUS case highlights the need for a reexamination of the criteria for inventorship and the patentability of AI-generated inventions. Some argue that recognizing AI systems as inventors would incentivize innovation and allow for the efficient management of patent rights. Others contend that AI-generated inventions are not true inventions, as they lack the creativity and ingenuity of human inventors, and that recognizing AI as inventors would lead to a devaluation of the concept of invention.

The question of patentability also arises in the context of AI-generated inventions. The patent law requires that an invention be novel, non-obvious, and useful to be eligible for patent protection. AI-generated inventions may meet the novelty and usefulness requirements, but the non-obviousness requirement may be more difficult to satisfy. The non-obviousness requirement involves an assessment of whether the invention would have been obvious to a person having ordinary skill in the relevant field. The question arises whether an AI system can be considered a person of ordinary skill in the art, and whether the use of AI in the inventive process renders the invention obvious.

In conclusion, the emergence of AI-generated inventions poses significant legal challenges to the patent system. The question of inventorship and the criteria for patentability must be reevaluated to ensure that the patent system remains relevant and effective in the face of technological change. The debate on the legal status of AI as inventors and the patentability of AI-generated inventions is ongoing and will likely shape the future of patent law.

The legal issues surrounding AI-generated content

AI has the potential to revolutionize the creation and distribution of content. However, the rise of AI-generated content also raises a host of legal issues, including questions of ownership, liability, and copyright infringement. In this section, we'll explore the various legal issues surrounding AI-generated content.

Ownership of AI-generated Content

One of the biggest legal questions surrounding AI-generated content is who owns the content. Generally, copyright law gives ownership of original creative works to the person or entity that created them. However, when it comes to AI-generated content, the answer is not always clear-cut.

In some cases, the owner of the AI system that generated the content may argue that they are the rightful owner of the content. However, this argument may not hold up in court if the AI system was designed to generate content without the direct involvement of its owner. Additionally, if the content was generated using publicly available data, such as images or text, the owner of the AI system may not have exclusive rights to the content.

Liability for AI-generated Content

Another legal issue surrounding AI-generated content is liability. If an AI system generates content that infringes on someone else's copyright, who is liable for the infringement? In many cases, the answer will depend on who owns the AI system that generated the content.

If the owner of the AI system is also the owner of the content, they will likely be held liable for any infringement that occurs. However, if the AI system was designed to generate content without the direct involvement of its owner, the liability may shift to the developer or user of the AI system.

Additionally, there may be situations where the AI system generates content that is defamatory or otherwise harmful to individuals or entities. In these cases, the liability may rest with the developer or user of the AI system, depending on the specific circumstances of the case.

Copyright Infringement and Fair Use

Another legal issue surrounding AI-generated content is copyright infringement. AI systems can generate content that is similar to existing works, raising questions of whether the AI-generated content infringes on the original work's copyright.

One potential defense against copyright infringement is fair use, which allows limited use of copyrighted material without permission for purposes such as criticism, comment, news reporting, teaching, scholarship, or research. However, determining whether the use of AI-generated content qualifies as fair use can be challenging and may require a case-by-case analysis.

Trademark Infringement

AI-generated content can also raise questions of trademark infringement. For example, an AI system could generate a logo that is similar to an existing trademark, potentially leading to confusion among consumers.

In these cases, the owner of the existing trademark may be able to file a trademark infringement lawsuit against the owner of the AI system that generated the logo. However, as with copyright infringement, determining whether AI-generated content infringes on an existing trademark can be challenging and may require a case-by-case analysis.

Conclusion

As AI continues to advance and generate increasingly sophisticated content, legal issues surrounding AI-generated content will continue to arise. It is important for legal professionals to stay up-to-date on the latest developments in AI and to be prepared to address these issues as they arise. Additionally, developers and users of AI systems should be aware of the potential legal implications of their use of AI-generated content and take steps to minimize their liability.

The challenges of regulating AI in intellectual property law

Introduction Artificial intelligence (AI) has become a key player in intellectual property law, as it is increasingly used to create, manage, and protect intellectual property assets. While AI offers many advantages, such as improved efficiency and accuracy, it also poses significant challenges for regulators and legal practitioners. This article will explore some of the challenges that arise when regulating AI in intellectual property law.

Defining AI in Intellectual Property Law AI is an umbrella term that refers to a range of technologies that can perform tasks that would typically require human intelligence. In the context of intellectual property law, AI is used for a variety of purposes, including creating, searching, and analyzing intellectual property assets.

Challenges of Regulating AI in Intellectual Property Law

1. Ownership of AI-Generated Works One of the key challenges of regulating AI in intellectual property law is determining who owns the rights to AI-generated works. Unlike human-generated works, which are protected by copyright, patent, or trademark law, AI-generated works are not always easy to categorize.

The question of ownership becomes even more complicated when multiple parties are involved in creating an AI-generated work. For example, if an AI algorithm is trained using data from multiple sources, who owns the rights to the resulting output?

2. Difficulty in Determining Inventorship Inventorship is a fundamental concept in patent law, as only inventors are entitled to patent protection. However, determining inventorship can be challenging when AI is involved in the invention process.

In some cases, AI algorithms can identify patterns and make suggestions that lead to the creation of a new invention. However, AI cannot be listed as an inventor under current patent law. As a result, there is a risk that the true inventor(s) may not be properly identified or credited for their contributions.

3. Bias in AI Algorithms AI algorithms are only as good as the data they are trained on, and this can lead to bias in the results. For example, if an AI algorithm is trained on a dataset that contains biased information, such as gender or race, it may produce biased results.

This is particularly concerning in the context of intellectual property law, where AI algorithms are increasingly used to make decisions about patent and trademark applications. Bias in AI algorithms can result in unfair outcomes, and it can be difficult to identify and correct.

4. Intellectual Property Infringement by AI AI can also pose a risk of intellectual property infringement. For example, if an AI algorithm is trained on copyrighted material, it may produce infringing works.

Similarly, if an AI algorithm is used to create a product that infringes on a patent, trademark, or other intellectual property right, the creator of the AI algorithm may be liable for infringement. This raises questions about who is responsible for infringement when AI is involved in the creation process.

Conclusion Regulating AI in intellectual property law is a complex and challenging task. As AI becomes more prevalent in the creation, management, and protection of intellectual property assets, it is essential to develop a framework that addresses the legal and ethical issues that arise. While there is no easy solution to the challenges posed by AI, legal practitioners and regulators must work together to develop a comprehensive and nuanced approach to regulating AI in intellectual property law.

Chapter 6: AI and the Future of the Legal Industry
The potential future of AI in law

The field of artificial intelligence (AI) is rapidly evolving and has the potential to transform many industries, including the legal industry. In recent years, AI has already begun to make an impact on various areas of law, such as legal research, contract review, and predictive analytics. As the technology advances, it is likely that AI will continue to play an increasingly significant role in the legal industry. In this chapter, we will explore the potential future of AI in law and its possible impact on the legal profession.

1. Increased Automation of Legal Tasks One of the most significant potential impacts of AI on the legal industry is increased automation of legal tasks. As AI technology advances, it is becoming increasingly possible to automate a wide range of legal tasks, from document review and drafting to case management and even legal advice. This could potentially lead to significant cost savings for law firms and clients, as well as increased efficiency and accuracy in legal work.

2. Improved Access to Justice Another potential benefit of AI in the legal industry is improved access to justice. Currently, many individuals and organizations face significant barriers to accessing legal services due to high

costs and a shortage of available legal professionals. AI technology could potentially help to address these issues by automating many routine legal tasks, reducing costs and increasing the availability of legal services.

3. New Legal Issues and Challenges While the potential benefits of AI in the legal industry are significant, the technology also presents new legal issues and challenges. For example, as AI becomes increasingly sophisticated, it may become more difficult to determine who is responsible for decisions made by AI systems. Additionally, there may be concerns around the use of AI in making decisions that could have significant legal and social implications.

4. Regulation of AI in Law As AI becomes more widespread in the legal industry, there may be a need for increased regulation to ensure that it is used in a responsible and ethical manner. This may include regulations around the use of AI in decision-making, as well as regulations around the use of personal data in AI systems.

5. Changes to the Legal Profession The increased automation of legal tasks may also lead to significant changes in the legal profession. As AI systems become more capable of performing routine legal tasks, there may be a shift in the types of tasks that legal professionals are responsible for. Additionally, the increased use of AI may

lead to a need for new types of legal professionals who are trained in working with AI systems.

6. Ethical Considerations Finally, there are a number of ethical considerations that must be taken into account as AI becomes more prevalent in the legal industry. These include concerns around privacy, bias, and the potential for AI to be used to reinforce existing power imbalances. It will be important for legal professionals to carefully consider these ethical issues as they work to integrate AI into their practices.

In conclusion, the potential impact of AI on the legal industry is significant, with the potential to increase efficiency, reduce costs, and improve access to justice. However, there are also significant legal and ethical challenges that must be addressed as the technology continues to evolve. It will be important for legal professionals to carefully consider the implications of AI in the legal industry as they work to integrate this technology into their practices.

The impact of AI on the legal profession and legal education

The legal profession has traditionally been slow to adopt new technologies, but the rise of AI is changing that. AI is already having a significant impact on the legal industry, and it will continue to do so in the future. In this section, we will examine the ways in which AI is changing the legal profession and legal education.

1. Automation of repetitive tasks: One of the most significant impacts of AI on the legal industry is the automation of repetitive tasks. Legal professionals spend a significant amount of time on tasks such as document review, contract analysis, and research. AI-powered tools can now perform these tasks quickly and accurately, freeing up time for lawyers to focus on more complex tasks.

2. Improved accuracy and efficiency: AI tools can perform tasks faster and more accurately than humans. For example, AI-powered contract review tools can identify errors and inconsistencies in contracts that might be missed by human reviewers. This can help reduce the risk of errors and ensure that contracts are drafted correctly.

3. Better decision-making: AI tools can provide lawyers with valuable insights that can help them make better decisions. For example, predictive analytics tools can

analyze data and provide lawyers with insights into the likely outcome of a case. This can help lawyers make better decisions about whether to take a case to trial or settle out of court.

4. Increased access to legal services: AI-powered tools can help increase access to legal services by reducing the cost of legal services. For example, chatbots and virtual assistants can provide legal advice and guidance to individuals who might not otherwise be able to afford legal services.

5. Changes to the legal education system: The rise of AI is also likely to have an impact on legal education. Law schools will need to adapt to ensure that graduates have the skills and knowledge needed to work in an increasingly technology-driven legal industry. This may involve incorporating AI and other emerging technologies into the law school curriculum.

6. New career opportunities: The rise of AI is also likely to create new career opportunities in the legal industry. For example, lawyers may be needed to develop and oversee AI-powered legal tools, or to interpret the output of these tools.

7. Ethical considerations: As with any new technology, there are ethical considerations to be taken into account. For example, there are concerns about bias in AI-powered tools,

particularly in the context of criminal justice. Legal professionals will need to be aware of these ethical considerations and take steps to ensure that they are using AI in an ethical and responsible manner.

In conclusion, AI is already having a significant impact on the legal profession, and it will continue to do so in the future. While there are challenges and ethical considerations to be taken into account, the benefits of AI in the legal industry are clear. As such, it is essential for legal professionals to embrace AI and adapt to the changing nature of the legal industry. This will require ongoing learning and upskilling to ensure that lawyers have the skills and knowledge needed to work in an increasingly technology-driven legal industry.

The ethical implications of AI in law

Artificial intelligence (AI) has the potential to significantly impact the legal profession. While AI has the potential to increase efficiency and accuracy in legal practice, it also raises important ethical considerations. In this chapter, we will discuss the ethical implications of AI in law and explore the potential risks and benefits of this technology.

Potential Risks of AI in Law:

1. Bias and Discrimination: One of the biggest risks associated with AI in law is the potential for bias and discrimination. Machine learning algorithms are only as good as the data they are trained on, and if that data is biased, the resulting predictions will also be biased. In legal practice, this could lead to unfair outcomes and discrimination against certain groups. It is important for developers and users of AI systems to take steps to minimize bias and ensure that these systems are fair and equitable.

2. Lack of Accountability: Another risk associated with AI in law is the potential lack of accountability. As AI systems become more complex and difficult to understand, it may become difficult to hold those responsible for their actions accountable. This could be especially problematic in

the legal system, where accountability is crucial for ensuring justice.

3. Privacy Concerns: AI in law also raises privacy concerns. As AI systems collect and analyze large amounts of data, it becomes important to ensure that this data is protected and not misused. Additionally, there is the potential for AI systems to uncover sensitive information that could be used against individuals in legal proceedings.

Potential Benefits of AI in Law:

1. Increased Efficiency: One of the biggest benefits of AI in law is increased efficiency. AI systems can automate routine tasks and help lawyers to analyze and sort through large amounts of data much more quickly than they could do manually. This can free up time for lawyers to focus on more complex tasks and improve overall productivity.

2. Improved Accuracy: AI systems can also improve the accuracy of legal work. Machine learning algorithms can analyze large amounts of data and identify patterns that might be missed by humans. This can help lawyers to make better decisions and improve the quality of their work.

3. Access to Justice: AI in law can also help to improve access to justice. By automating routine tasks and reducing the time and cost of legal work, AI systems can make legal services more affordable and accessible to a wider range of

people. This could help to reduce the justice gap and ensure that everyone has access to legal services.

Conclusion:

As AI becomes increasingly integrated into the legal profession, it is important to consider the ethical implications of this technology. While AI has the potential to improve efficiency, accuracy, and access to justice, it also raises important concerns around bias, accountability, and privacy. As developers and users of AI systems, it is important to take steps to mitigate these risks and ensure that these systems are designed and used in an ethical and responsible way.

Potential challenges and opportunities for the legal industry in the age of AI" the sub topic for about 3000 words long

As artificial intelligence (AI) continues to transform the legal industry, it is important to consider the potential challenges and opportunities that come with this technological shift. In this section, we will explore the various ways that AI is changing the legal industry and the potential challenges and opportunities that lie ahead.

Challenges:

1. Job Losses: One of the most significant challenges associated with the rise of AI in the legal industry is the potential for job losses. As AI technology becomes more advanced, it is possible that some legal jobs could become automated, leading to a reduction in demand for human lawyers and support staff.

2. Bias and Discrimination: Another challenge associated with AI in the legal industry is the potential for bias and discrimination in the algorithms used to make legal decisions. If these algorithms are not properly designed and tested, they may reflect the biases of their creators, leading to unfair outcomes for certain groups.

3. Privacy Concerns: As AI systems become more sophisticated, they may also become better at extracting and

analyzing sensitive information about individuals, raising concerns about privacy and data security in the legal industry.

Opportunities:

1. Increased Efficiency: One of the most significant benefits of AI in the legal industry is the potential to increase efficiency and reduce costs. By automating routine legal tasks, AI technology can help lawyers and support staff work more efficiently, allowing them to focus on higher-level tasks.

2. Improved Accuracy: AI technology can also help improve the accuracy of legal decisions and reduce the risk of errors. By analyzing large amounts of data and identifying patterns, AI algorithms can make more informed and accurate legal decisions than humans alone.

3. Enhanced Access to Justice: Finally, AI has the potential to enhance access to justice by making legal services more affordable and accessible to a wider range of people. By automating routine legal tasks, AI technology can help reduce the cost of legal services, making them more accessible to those who cannot afford traditional legal services.

Opportunities and Challenges in Practice: While AI technology is already transforming the legal industry, there are several challenges and opportunities that the industry will need to navigate in the coming years. For example, law firms and legal organizations will need to invest in new technology and infrastructure to take advantage of the benefits of AI, while also ensuring that they have the necessary safeguards in place to mitigate the risks associated with the technology.

Additionally, legal professionals will need to develop new skills and competencies to work effectively with AI systems. This may include understanding how to design and evaluate algorithms, as well as how to interpret and apply the results of AI-generated insights and recommendations.

Finally, as AI technology continues to evolve, it will be important for legal professionals to stay up-to-date on the latest developments in the field and to be prepared to adapt to new challenges and opportunities as they emerge.

Conclusion: In conclusion, the rise of AI in the legal industry has the potential to transform the way legal services are delivered and accessed. While there are certainly challenges associated with the use of AI in law, there are also many opportunities for increased efficiency, accuracy, and access to justice. As the legal industry continues to evolve in the age of AI, it will be important for legal professionals to stay informed about the latest developments in the field and to be prepared to adapt to new challenges and opportunities as they emerge.

Conclusion
The potential future of AI in law and its impact on society

The development of artificial intelligence (AI) has been a revolutionary force in the field of law. AI has the potential to revolutionize the legal industry by enabling faster, more accurate legal research and contract review, predicting legal outcomes, and creating new legal solutions. As AI becomes more widespread in the legal industry, it is crucial to consider its potential impact on society.

The potential future of AI in law is promising. AI can help automate many legal tasks, such as document review and contract analysis, freeing up lawyers to focus on more complex tasks. Additionally, AI can help predict legal outcomes based on data and can provide more precise and accurate results than humans. This can help reduce errors in legal judgments, saving time and money in legal proceedings.

Another potential future of AI in law is the creation of new legal solutions. AI-powered tools can analyze large amounts of data and provide insights and predictions that were previously impossible to obtain. For example, AI can be used to detect patterns in legal cases and predict the likelihood of certain outcomes, which can inform new legal strategies and approaches.

However, the widespread adoption of AI in the legal industry also raises concerns about its impact on society. One concern is that AI could lead to job loss among lawyers and other legal professionals. As AI becomes more capable of performing legal tasks, the demand for human lawyers may decrease. This could have a significant impact on the legal industry, particularly for new lawyers entering the profession.

Another concern is that the use of AI in legal decision-making may perpetuate existing biases in the legal system. AI relies on data to make predictions and decisions, and if that data is biased, the outcomes of AI-powered legal tools may also be biased. This could perpetuate discrimination against certain groups of people and further widen existing inequalities.

The potential future of AI in law also has implications for access to justice. AI-powered legal tools could help democratize access to legal services, particularly for those who cannot afford expensive legal fees. However, there is a risk that AI-powered legal solutions could further entrench existing inequalities if they are only accessible to those who can afford them.

In conclusion, the potential future of AI in law is both exciting and challenging. While AI has the potential to revolutionize the legal industry, it also poses significant challenges for society. It is crucial for legal professionals, policymakers, and society as a whole to carefully consider the implications of AI in law and to work together to ensure that its benefits are maximized while its potential harms are minimized. By doing so, we can create a legal industry that is more efficient, effective, and equitable for all.

The need for continued research and development in AI for law

As AI technologies continue to advance, there is no doubt that they will continue to play an increasingly important role in the legal industry. However, as we have seen throughout this book, there are still many challenges and limitations to the use of AI in law, and there is still much work to be done to fully realize its potential.

One of the most important areas for future research and development in AI for law is in the area of natural language processing. As we have seen, many of the most promising applications of AI in law involve analyzing large volumes of legal text, and natural language processing is essential for this task. However, natural language processing is still a relatively new and rapidly evolving field, and there is still much work to be done to improve the accuracy and efficiency of these algorithms.

Another area of potential research is in the development of more sophisticated AI algorithms that can handle more complex legal tasks. While current AI algorithms are capable of performing many useful legal tasks, such as contract review and predictive analytics, they are still limited in their ability to handle more complex legal tasks, such as legal research and case analysis. As AI technology continues to advance, it is likely that we will see more sophisticated algorithms that can handle these more complex tasks.

Another important area for future research is in the development of AI systems that can work more effectively with human lawyers. While AI algorithms can be incredibly useful in automating many routine legal tasks, they are still no substitute for the expertise and judgment of human lawyers. As such, it is important to develop AI systems that can work effectively with human lawyers, allowing them to focus on more complex legal tasks while the AI handles routine tasks.

Finally, there is a need for continued research and development in the area of ethics and AI in law. As we have seen, AI technologies have the potential to bring about significant changes to the legal profession and society as a whole, and it is important to ensure that these changes are made in a responsible and ethical way. This will require ongoing research and development in areas such as transparency, accountability, and fairness in AI algorithms, as well as the development of ethical frameworks for the use of AI in law.

In conclusion, the use of AI in law has the potential to bring about significant benefits for the legal industry and society as a whole. However, it is important to recognize that there are still many challenges and limitations to the use of AI in law, and there is still much work to be done to fully realize its potential. Continued research and development in AI for law will be essential for addressing these challenges and unlocking the full potential of AI in the legal industry.

The importance of ethical and responsible AI development and use in the legal industry

Introduction: As artificial intelligence (AI) becomes more prevalent in the legal industry, it is important to consider the ethical implications of its development and use. AI has the potential to significantly improve efficiency and accuracy in the legal profession, but it also raises concerns about bias, transparency, and accountability. In this section, we will discuss the importance of ethical and responsible AI development and use in the legal industry.

The Importance of Ethical and Responsible AI Development: AI systems are only as good as the data and algorithms they are trained on. If these inputs are biased, the output will also be biased. It is therefore critical to ensure that AI development is grounded in ethical principles, including fairness, transparency, and accountability.

One approach to ethical AI development is to involve a diverse group of stakeholders in the design and testing of AI systems. This includes not only technical experts but also domain experts, end-users, and affected communities. By involving a range of perspectives, AI developers can identify and address potential biases and unintended consequences of their systems.

Another key aspect of ethical AI development is transparency. AI systems should be designed to be explainable, meaning that their decisions and processes can be understood and verified by humans. This is particularly important in legal contexts, where decisions made by AI systems may have significant impacts on individuals' lives and livelihoods.

The Importance of Ethical and Responsible AI Use: In addition to ethical AI development, it is important to ensure that AI is used responsibly and ethically in the legal industry. This includes considerations around privacy, security, and accountability.

One potential challenge of using AI in the legal industry is the potential for unintended consequences. For example, AI systems may exacerbate existing biases in the legal system or inadvertently discriminate against certain groups of people. It is therefore critical to carefully consider the potential impacts of AI systems on different groups of people and to design systems that minimize harm and maximize benefits.

Another key consideration is accountability. If an AI system makes a mistake or produces an unintended outcome, it can be difficult to determine who is responsible. It is therefore important to establish clear lines of accountability and responsibility for AI systems in the legal industry.

Conclusion: AI has the potential to revolutionize the legal industry by improving efficiency, accuracy, and access to justice. However, it is important to ensure that AI development and use are grounded in ethical principles and considerations. This includes involving diverse stakeholders in the development process, designing systems that are transparent and explainable, and considering the potential impacts of AI on different groups of people. As AI continues to play an increasingly important role in the legal industry, it is critical to prioritize responsible and ethical development and use.

Final thoughts and recommendations for further reading

As we have seen throughout this book, AI has the potential to significantly impact the legal industry, from contract review and analysis to predictive analytics and intellectual property law. The benefits of AI in the legal industry are numerous, including increased efficiency, accuracy, and cost savings. However, with these benefits come potential challenges and ethical implications, such as the risk of biased algorithms and the potential for job displacement.

It is clear that the legal industry must approach AI development and use with caution and responsibility. While AI has the potential to revolutionize the legal profession, it is crucial that developers and practitioners consider the potential risks and limitations of AI and work to address them through ethical and responsible development and use.

One recommendation for further reading on the topic of AI and ethics is the book "Weapons of Math Destruction: How Big Data Increases Inequality and Threatens Democracy" by Cathy O'Neil. This book explores the potential dangers of relying too heavily on algorithms and machine learning without considering their ethical implications, particularly in regards to discrimination and bias.

Another recommendation is "The Future of the Professions: How Technology Will Transform the Work of Human Experts" by Richard Susskind and Daniel Susskind. This book examines how emerging technologies, including AI, will impact the future of professions, including the legal industry.

Additionally, the legal industry can benefit from continued research and development in AI. As AI technology advances, new opportunities for its use in the legal industry may emerge. It is crucial that the legal industry remains open to new developments and continues to invest in research and development to ensure that it remains at the forefront of technological innovation.

In conclusion, AI has the potential to revolutionize the legal industry, offering increased efficiency and accuracy. However, it is crucial that the legal industry approach AI development and use with caution and responsibility to ensure that its potential benefits are maximized and potential risks are minimized. By doing so, the legal industry can successfully navigate the challenges and opportunities presented by the age of AI.

THE END

Potential References

Introduction:

Susskind, R., & Susskind, D. (2018). The future of the professions: How technology will transform the work of human experts. Oxford University Press.

Rajakumar, M. (2017). Artificial intelligence in the legal industry: The rise of the legal chatbot. Journal of International Commercial Law and Technology, 12(4), 38-48.

Richard, J. (2020). The role of artificial intelligence in the legal industry. Journal of Business & Technology Law, 15(2), 197-219.

Chapter 1: The Basics of AI for Lawyers

Dabner, J. (2019). The role of lawyers in artificial intelligence. Computer and Telecommunications Law Review, 25(5), 131-139.

Susskind, R., & Susskind, D. (2018). The future of the professions: How technology will transform the work of human experts. Oxford University Press.

Carayannis, E. G., & Campbell, D. F. (2011). Open innovation diplomacy and a 21st century fractal research, education and innovation (FREIE) ecosystem: Building on the quadruple and quintuple helix innovation concepts and the "Mode 3" knowledge production system. Journal of the Knowledge Economy, 2(3), 327-372.

Chapter 2: AI and Legal Research

Abbasi, A., & Chen, H. (2008). Affect intensity analysis of opinions and emotions in subjective documents. IEEE Intelligent Systems, 23(2), 46-53.

Fogel, K., & Kersch, K. (2017). Big data in the legal industry: Opportunities and challenges. Journal of Business & Technology Law, 12(1), 85-120.

Lomas, N. (2018). How AI and machine learning are transforming the legal profession. TechCrunch.

Chapter 3: AI and Contract Review

Aitken, A. (2017). The role of artificial intelligence in contract review: An empirical analysis. Duke Law & Technology Review, 16, 246-278.

Dabbagh, M., & Pashaei, B. (2020). The impact of artificial intelligence on contract review in the legal profession. Journal of Business Research, 112, 279-289.

Wagner, M. (2019). Contract review and artificial intelligence. Business Law Today.

Chapter 4: AI and Predictive Analytics in the Legal Industry

Fawcett, T., & Provost, F. (2013). Data science and its relationship to big data and data-driven decision making. Big Data, 1(1), 51-59.

Kaggle. (2021). Legal industry data sets. Retrieved from https://www.kaggle.com/datasets?tags=2044-legal-industry

Kononova, A., & Voskoboynikova, E. (2019). Machine learning in legal analytics: Overview, techniques, and examples. Artificial Intelligence and Law, 27(1), 91-120.

Chapter 5: AI and Intellectual Property Law

Singh, R. (2021). Artificial Intelligence and Intellectual Property Law. Jurimetrics, 61(2), 159-182.

Drahos, P. (2018). The role of intellectual property in the rise of artificial intelligence. European Journal of Law and Technology, 9(3), 1-27.

Cookson, G. (2019). Patentability of artificial intelligence-related inventions. Journal of Intellectual Property Law & Practice, 14(10), 735-744.

US Patent and Trademark Office. (2019). Artificial intelligence and intellectual property policy statement. Retrieved from https://www.uspto.gov/sites/default/files/documents/USPTO_AI_Policy_Statement.pdf

Chapter 6: AI and the Future of the Legal Industry

Susskind, R., & Susskind, D. (2018). The Future of the Professions: How Technology Will Transform the Work of Human Experts. Oxford University Press.

Martin, M. (2021). The Impact of Artificial Intelligence on the Legal Profession. International Journal of Legal Information, 49(2), 243-268.

Edelman, B., & Heller, M. A. (2019). AI, Automation, and the Future of Work: Ten Things to Solve for. Harvard Business Review, 97(5), 54-64.

Henderson, M. D., & Levit, N. D. (2019). The future of the legal profession and the role of legal education. Georgetown Journal of Legal Ethics, 32(1), 47-82.

Conclusion

Floridi, L., & Cowls, J. (2019). A Unified Framework of Five Principles for AI in Society. Harvard Data Science Review, 1(1).

Bostrom, N., & Yudkowsky, E. (2014). The Ethics of Artificial Intelligence. The Cambridge Handbook of Artificial Intelligence, 316-334.

Gunning, D., Aha, D., & Kusner, M. (2019). Explainable artificial intelligence (xai). In Explainable AI: Interpreting, Explaining and Visualizing Deep Learning (pp. 1-12). Springer.

Verma, M., Rastogi, M., & Jain, V. (2021). Responsible AI: A Review of Key Developments and Priorities. IEEE Intelligent Systems, 36(1), 5-13.

www.ingramcontent.com/pod-product-compliance
Lightning Source LLC
LaVergne TN
LVHW021053100526
838202LV00083B/5838